Getting Your Dream Job

"The world makes way for the determined person"

I0164113

John Wanjora

Excellence Media
Nairobi, Kenya

Copyright © 2008, John Wanjora

First Published by Excellence Media

2008.

ISBN: 9966 - 7290 - 0 - 3

The names of people and institutions cited in this book are meant for illustrative purposes only, and should thus not be interpreted to mean any past, present or future state of being of any person or organisation.

Published in East Africa by
Excellence Media
Nairobi, Kenya.

Site: www.excellencemedia.co.nr

E-mail: excellencemedia@live.com

Dedication

For Phoebe Njambi, my loving wife and my greatest friend.
God brought us together to share in this wonderful love, hope and destiny. May we live to see the fulfilment of God's divine purpose for our home.

Introduction

Graduating from university or college with great certificates in the course of your dreams crowns your many years of hard work in school. Looking back to how far you've come in life, this might feel like a destiny in itself.

For this, you deserve everyone's congratulations! However, as you will realize soon, every major achievement signifies a new beginning, often a more important challenge. The essential task that awaits you now is finding an opportunity to put your skills into good use so as to earn a decent living. This book has been written to serve as a bridge, first to help you cross over from college to your first job, and second, after you've gained the necessary skills and experience, hand you over to the job of your dreams.

By saying this, I wouldn't like to overlook the fact that some people get on to their dream jobs immediately after college. These are the lucky few. For majority of graduates, as we shall see later in this book, the first job is often less than satisfying, which leads to craving for better opportunities either within the organization or elsewhere.

However, we must understand from the beginning that a less satisfying first job doesn't mean the same thing as what some people refer to as a 'useless job'. I might not have a good definition of a useless job. All I know is that depending on the organization that you will be working for, a first job – its level of satisfaction not withstanding - could give you the crucial foundation that you need in your career, and make an important stepping stone to the future that you've always seen through your mind's eye. You can read more on this in Chapter two (The Job Search and Application Process) and Chapter 11 (Now that you have a New Job).

Having said that, I understand that you could already be in a less satisfying job and you are raving to make a move to a better work environment. Maybe you even have a pen and paper in your hand and you want to write your CV or letter of application to the prospective employer. May be you have just a few moments before facing an interview panel, and so you have paused to check out what could be in this book for you. Rest assured that you've made a right decision, and the few moments you will spend with this book will soon prove a worthy investment.

In addition to giving you practical advice and accompanying examples on how to make your letters of application more persuasive, your CVs more effective in communicating your abilities to the employer, and how to face the interviewer with confidence, this book takes a unique approach by revealing to you the employer's considerations at every stage of the hiring process.

Understanding exactly what your prospective employer is looking for in a candidate will give you an opportunity to fine tune your presentation towards those requirements before meeting him or her. To give you a further unfair advantage over your competitors, this book will show you how to tweak the knobs in order to maximise on your chances of securing the job.

Inside this book you will find great solutions to many other job search-related problems. Feel free to move from one chapter to another as you wish – not necessarily in the order presented here. Many people have found *Getting Your Dream*

Job a blessing in their job search and career progression, and I hope that you will also find it so. If you're looking for your first job, or if you're seeking greener pastures elsewhere, remember what the Bible says, that crying may prevail through the night but joy comes in the morning. May the Lord bless your going out and your coming back, Amen!

Ritah Mutuku

Contents

1

The Modern Job Market

"I have learned that success is to be measured not so much by the position that one has reached in life as by the obstacles which he has overcome while trying to succeed."

- Booker T. Washington

For beginners, wonderful jobs in super-motivating environments are hard to come by, and competition for the few opportunities that show up is often cutthroat. Getting a job in some of the high flying organisations can get personal, sometimes degenerating into a question of who you know up the organisation's hierarchy.

Despite this, the most important fact that the employer wants to establish is whether you can fit easily into the organisation and make a contribution that exceeds the amount of pay that you stand to earn. It therefore matters less to the employer how you got to learn about the job opportunity – whether through the media, social contacts, etc, provided the job gets done to the given specifications, within the given time limit and within the agreed budget.

The rate at which the modern job market is evolving is astounding. New fields of professionalism are springing up by day, much at the same rate that some older professions, previously held in high esteem, are becoming redundant.

There were times, for instance, when being a secretary was the in thing, and most managers had a company driver too. But those days are forever gone, and most contemporary managers prepare their own documents, reducing opportunities for secretaries, and drive themselves around – which means dwindling opportunities for company drivers.

Focus is thus shifting rapidly towards newer frontiers such as Information and Communication Technology (ICT), and the job seeker hasn't been spared by this revolution either. Emergence of electronic resume databases such as *myjobeye. com*, as well as the growing necessity for anyone seeking employment to have a functional E-mail address and a mobile phone number is enough proof that times have changed.

Indeed, most applications for jobs, among other forms of official correspondence, are now sent through E-mail, which has proved cheaper and more efficient for both applicants and hiring organisations. To all this, add the fact that job searching has evolved into a project - requiring clear objectives, a realistic budget and a time frame within which it should be accomplished.

Need for Planning
To guarantee success, it is important that you clarify what you want to achieve in your job search. This includes setting a realistic salary target, location – whether you want to work near or away from home, besides being lucid on the conditions under which you wish to work – whether permanent and pensionable, contract, or temporary, among other considerations. Without such a plan, you can end up selling your skills at a cost that is by far less than their actual market value.

The cost of printing and sending your CVs and letters of application, attending interviews and making phone calls has to be met somehow. In order to gain proper control over your financial investment in the job search process, you need to come up with a budget, based on a carefully selected list of possible employers. This is important whether you are meeting your own job search related expenses or you have someone else footing the bills.

Every realistic project must have a time frame. A well designed schedule of implementation will point out to you specific point where you can pause, look back and gauge what you have achieved so far. It also gives you a rare chance to reflect on the experiences that you have undergone and see what needs to be done differently in order to achieve your desired objectives. Otherwise, the search for the dream job becomes a vague, expensive, time consuming and tiresome venture.

Do not despise SMEs
As the wave of industrialisation and technological advancement sweeps across the country, some of the hitherto undermined employers, especially small and medium enterprises (SMEs), are becoming more rewarding than major corporations.

At the same time, the prestige that once came from working for trans-nationals is fading fast, thanks to the massive retrenchments that they have carried out over the past decade. Indeed, many foreign owned companies have moved their manufacturing facilities to countries where production costs are lower, leaving behind only their marketing functions. With these negative developments, focus for job seekers has now turned towards local smaller organisations that are seeking expertise for rapid growth.

That nondescript SMEs can grow into remarkable corporations is best illustrated by the case of Equity Bank.

A few years ago, few graduates would have given thought to Equity Building Society as a first line employer.

Today, the once small building society has transformed into one of the leading commercial banks in Kenya. Equity is now known for high levels of professionalism in service delivery, and has become a great attraction for experienced bankers even from the Central Bank of Kenya. The working conditions for Equity employees are also miles ahead of what they used to be when it operated as a regional-based micro-finance institution.

Finally, looking at the reputation and future direction of the organisation that you wish to work for isn't a bad idea. The wise will tell you that joining a sinking firm can dent your CV and limit your chances of career growth. It's a fact that most employers have an unspoken bias towards qualified candidates coming from the more successful organisations compared to their counterparts from collapsing institutions.

The assumption here is simple: candidates from successful organisations stand to bring tested and proved work practises, which their counterparts from sinking institutions might be badly in need of.

2

The Job Search Process

"The only place you'll find success before work is in the dictionary." – Mary B. Smith

If you have been searching for a new job for some time, you must have realised that the process of getting one in any field – be it in medicine, law, ICT or teaching, is basically the same:

A vacancy arises in an organisation and the employer finds it necessary to fill it. Some of the reasons why vacancies arise include: a new business coming up; retirement; death; resignation or transfer of employees; as well as business expansion. So, the employer advertises the post in-house, in the media or through any other channel of choice.

Upon getting word that such a vacancy exists, suitably qualified candidates send in their applications enclosing their CVs for consideration.

Upon reading and reviewing the applications, the employer shortlists those with the right combination of skills and experience, and invites them for a single or series of interviews. From the interview results, the employer offers the job to the most qualified candidate.

Should the candidate accept the offer, the recruitment process for that post ends. But should he or she reject the offer, the employer moves on to the second most qualified candidate according to the interview results.

From the above description we find that the recruitment process has two major players in it: the employer and the applicant. Each of these comes to the negotiating table with a different motive as we are about to discover below.

Employer's Motive
The employer's chief concern is hiring a candidate with the best combination of skills and experience to handle the job in question. Once the right candidate has been found, the next question becomes whether his productivity will exceed the amount of pay that he will receive from the company. Reason for this second consideration is that the company can only benefit by hiring an individual whose contribution leaves some profit once his pay is deducted. Otherwise, the company will only be taking in a liability that it can do without!

On this account, you might possess the required level of skills and years of experience, but lose out on the job if you demand a pay that is too high for the task.

Different companies in different stages of growth give different pay packages for similar jobs, but it wouldn't be wise to base your salary quotation on what your friends are earning elsewhere. If from your self evaluation you believe that you have already met the first criterion of skills and experience, the next step now is researching the company's salary range and preparing to give your quotation accordingly at the interview.

Applicant's Motive
As an applicant, you are interested in a job that will pay you well to afford a decent living. Besides, you need an employer

who will give you job security and a working environment that is conducive for both your personal and professional development. When these basic requirements are met, you can work confidently and advance in life.

In reality however, most fresh graduates are disappointed that their first jobs lack some or all the above qualities. A major reason for this is that most of the new opportunities arise in start-up ventures which might not be well endowed to offer great chances for advancement.

A second reason is that in the relatively well established organisations, most job opportunities arise high up the corporate ladder or at the middle levels, and either require high qualifications, or are filled through internal promotions. This leaves new vacancies only at the lower rungs of the ladder, and this happens to be the place where most newcomers begin.

Importance of a First Job

Nonetheless, a first job – its level of satisfaction not withstanding - is important as it will enable you to learn the ropes and gather the expertise that is required to handle higher positions. A second importance is that the job will give you an opportunity to expand your social network. These are the people that you can run to later in life for your own rescue or when referring someone else looking for a job. In many ways, a first job is like a kindergarten - an important beginning but hardly ever your career destiny.

Unaware of this fact, some applicants hop from one employer to another seeking heaven, and thus fail to develop the necessary discipline to work and solve problems. Others, after hopping endlessly and losing the chance to establish themselves in a career, despair and approach the job market as underdogs. They end up doubting their skills, abilities and talents, and sell themselves off to any willing employer at the price of a meal. When they finally wake up to reality, they find that their more patient colleagues have either risen to senior management positions or are happily running their own businesses.

Ideally, patience is an important virtue in the quest for your dream job, though it isn't the same thing as accepting slavery at the workplace. Your relationship with your employer should be a contract between two equal parties: The employer needs the skills and services that you have to offer, while you, on the other hand, need the job in order to earn an honest living from your skills.

Seven Steps to Getting the Job

From your perspective as an applicant, the job search and application process can be broken down into the following seven convenient stages which form the bulwark of this book:

1. Career exploration.

2. The job search.

3. Responding to adverts.

4. The actual application.

5. Preparation for the interview.

6. The interview.

7. Follow up

Career Exploration

This is the crucial stage where one decides on which line of profession to pursue in life. Professional training can be expensive and time consuming, hence the need for caution when making this decision. In order to guarantee that one trains for the best career, this decision should be made early in life, preferably while one is still in high school.

However, at this level, the assumption is that you made the best decision on which career to pursue, trained for it, and that all you need now is a chance to make a living out of your trade.

The Job Search
Now that you have the necessary training, the next step becomes looking for places where jobs in your profession are advertised. Such include newspapers, the Internet, professional journals and magazines, public notice boards, job placement bureaux and word of mouth.

Once you have identified a number of organisations that need someone with qualifications similar to yours, you need to sit down and assess which one presents the best deal for you. Remember that you have some specific objectives that you hope to achieve in your job search. Before wasting your time and money on an employer who doesn't deserve you, it's only polite that you put them all to test. This will among other things, help you in setting priorities just in case they all send you positive responses. Below are sample questions that could help you in evaluating an employer:

• What is the organisation's reputation on how it treats its employees? Some companies are known to give little if any regard to the welfare of their staff, while others recognise their workforce as their most important resource, and thus respect and treat them well. If you value yourself, you will most likely opt for the latter kind of employer.

• Does the job offer prospects for personal and career growth or is it a dead end? This is an important question as it will help you determine how long you can hope to remain with the employer. While some organisations have clearly defined career paths for their employees, most of the smaller ones have specific positions rigidly held by specific individuals or relatives. Such practises hold back everyone else's career progression, and prior research should help you know if your prospective employer practises this. If anything, this kind of organisations is only suitable for beginners, after which they can leave for greener pastures once they accumulate the level of work experience required for better jobs elsewhere.

• Is the amount of pay offered for people at my level of skills and experience acceptable for the amount of work that I will be required to do? It's only volunteers and interns who work for no pay. You can improve your understanding of the employer's financial standing by enquiring from people who are conversant with the organisation.

• Will I be covered by any health insurance or retirement benefit schemes such as NHIF and NSSF? (Both organisations have transformed and now accept individual contributions from both the employed and the self employed).

• Will I be required to work for long hours including weekends; will this be counted as overtime, and at what rate of pay per hour?

• Will I be required to relocate closer to the place of work? This question has gained new significance especially after the ethnic violence that erupted after the December 2007 General Elections. Since then, some people would prefer to work in areas which they consider safe enough for them – at least in the mean time.

• Do I know the name and address of the organisation's human resources manager? This is one question that sets apart real job seekers from jokers. After you've settled on the list of organisations to approach for the job, you need to know, by name, the people to whom you will be addressing your application documents. If you don't know them already, plan to call the company and enquire.

In order to elicit interest and take full advantage of each encounter with a prospective employer, you need to prove that you know them well. You need to find out details such as what services or products they offer, their management structures, their competitors in the market, and any other relevant information you can lay your hands on regarding the organisation and the job you are applying for.

Good sources of such information include talking to the company's employees; reading professional journals; company magazines; business publications in the field within which the organisation falls; as well as browsing the company's website on the net.

Besides letting you into what kind of organisation you will be dealing with, this kind of search will give you deeper insight into the kind of person the employer wants.

The Actual Application
This is the stage where you put together all your relevant background information, including your academic and professional qualifications and letters of recommendation, or all the evidence that convinces you that you are the most qualified person to fill the vacancy. This is the information that you need to compile a powerful CV and cover letter, which you then send to each prospective employer. Note that each employer requires a unique CV and cover letter tailored to meet his or her specific needs as outlined in the job advert.

When a letter of application is sent accompanied by a CV, it is referred to as a cover letter. While the CV carries the details of your qualifications and achievements, the purpose of the cover letter is to express your interest in the job, to introduce your CV, and to ask for an interview.

Preparation for the Interview

Should any of the employers find your combination of skills and experience suitable for the job, he will send you mail inviting you to an interview. This correspondence should give specific details concerning the date, venue and time of the interview.

A good way to start preparing for the interview is by further researching on the employer. Rather than gathering general information, the focus now should be on things such as the organisation's culture, specific requirements for the job that you are preparing for, and virtually any other details that could enable you present yourself as the best candidate for the job.

If you have never talked to any employee of the company, this is the time to befriend them; as such a social investment will pay off handsomely soon. In addition, search on the Internet and talk to people who hold similar positions either with the employer or elsewhere. This will update you on the specific duties, responsibilities, challenges as well as opportunities associated with the job.

With this backgrounds information, you will be able to demonstrate, during the interview, that you understand the heights and depths of the job. It will also enable you to show convincingly how your set of skills and experience can be applied in a practical way to achieve the objectives set for that position.

The Interview

This is where you finally meet with the prospective employer to assess your suitability in filling the vacancy. It is from this interaction that the employer will finally decide on who to hire out of all participating candidates.

The Follow Up

This comes after the interview. Courtesy requires that you call or write a thank you letter or e-mail to the interviewer(s) expressing your gratitude for having taken their time to interview you. In this communication, you should also express optimism that the employer will indeed consider you for the job.

Chapter

3

Sources of Information on Jobs

*"Things may come to those who wait, but only what's
left by those who hustle." - Abraham Lincoln*

Information concerning available job opportunities can be
gotten from a number of sources, though here will explore the
four most common ones:

The Mass Media
This is the most common channel through which organizations
inform the public of their intention to hire. The *Daily Nation*
and *The Standard,* Kenya's leading dailies, have set apart
Fridays as the day when they publish the bulk of new job
openings. Magazines and professional journals can also be
good sources of information on available opportunities and on
career progression.

Electronic media comprising largely the radio and TV, as
well as subscribing to mobile phone job alerts are also great
sources of information on emerging opportunities.

The Internet
Today, most organizations have websites where they post
their vacancies. The Public Service Commission, the recruiting

agency for the Government, has also gone online and one can apply for civil service jobs at *www.publicservice.go.ke.*

For those seeking part time jobs such as writing of university term papers and other document preparation services, *www.guru.com* and *www.elance.com* can make a good starting point. It should however be stated that the level of fraud on the net is alarming, especially in the area of jobs that can be done at home.

For this reason, you should exercise discretion when filling in sensitive details such as your bank account, credit and debit card numbers online. Also, bear in mind that most of the genuine websites advertising project -based jobs do not ask for subscription fees, neither do they require you to pay for anything upfront. Instead, they are the ones who pay you once you deliver services for their clients as per the agreement.

Social Contacts

While some big companies have regulations requiring them to advertise their vacancies in the media, smaller ones don't have this as a necessary condition, and so prefer to source their staff through social networks. By talking to people in different organizations, you can get to learn about many emerging opportunities even before they are openly advertised.

Take it upon yourself to build a network of well connected friends, starting with your relatives and former classmates. These can provide you with useful contacts of people you may reach out to in your job search. Even after securing the job, maintain a record of these contacts as they will prove useful in future when researching on different companies or when seeking greener pastures.

Job Placement Agencies

Most local universities have job placement offices or student organisations which occasionally organise forums to bring together prospective employers and graduating students. These can form a good starting point for job-hunting for college university graduates.

Outside learning institutions, there are a number of job placement agencies where employers send their requests for qualified candidates whenever vacancies arise in their organizations. A good number of these advertise their services or vacancies that they are seeking to fill on behalf of their clients at Adpost notice boards outside Odeon Cinema in Nairobi.

Most of such agencies require you to pay a certain amount of subscription fee for their services. Alternatively, they may enter into an agreement with your employer so that a certain amount of money is deducted from your salary to settle the bill for having used their services.

Some job placement agencies such as *myjobeye.com* and *casulajobskenya.com* offer online services too, whereby you can view updated vacancies every day and select which ones to apply for. However, some online services will only disclose full details of the job once you have paid the subscription fees.

The best thing about job placement agencies is that besides matching you with prospective employers, they can also assist you in fine tuning your application documents to meet the specific requirements of various employers in their database.

The better agencies go an extra mile and assist you in preparing for interviews to ensure that you succeed. In order to increase your chances of landing a nice job soon, you can subscribe to as many agencies as you can afford. But given that no area of service provision is immune to fraud, it is important that you first establish the credibility and reputation of each agency before subscribing to their services.

Irrespective of the channel through which the chance to meet your employer comes, remember that searching for a job is entirely a communication process. There is need for you to sharpen your skills in both oral and written communication if you hope to shine in this process.

4

How to Write Compelling Application Letters

"You can have brilliant ideas, but if you can't get them across, your ideas won't get you anywhere."
- Lee Iacoca

"Don't judge each day by the harvest you reap, but by the seeds you plant." – Robert Louis Stevenson

Essentially, a letter of application should be brief and to the point. In terms of length, it should not exceed a single page. And to make it more effective in serving its purpose, the letter should meet the following three objectives:

1. Express interest in the job for which you are applying.

2. Briefly show how your background and work experience qualify you for the job.

3. Ask for an interview.

As we found out in earlier chapters, when the application letter accompanies a CV, the letter is referred to as a cover letter. Letters of application can be sent under two circumstances:

• When responding to a job advertisement. This is also referred to as solicited application.

• When no job opening exists at all, but the applicant sends the letter to introduce himself to the employer. This is also referred to as unsolicited application. In either case, the chief purpose in sending the application is to make the prospective employer interested in your skills and capabilities so that he may invite you for an interview.

A letter of application takes the usual format of an official letter. It has the sender's name, address and the date sent on the one right hand side, and the name and address of the recipient to the left.

The letter should be addressed to either the hiring authority for the position that you are interested in, or to the company's human resource manager. In addition, you should give the letter a more personal touch by including the recipient's full name in the salutation, e.g., *Dear Mr. Davis Wekesa*. In case you are not sure of the person's name or spelling, call the company and find out. Other details that should go into the letter include:

• The purpose for which you are sending the letter or title of the job you are interested in. This is usually contained in the reference section that comes immediately after salutation.

• A brief highlight of your skills and a direct invitation of the manager to read the attached CV. If your qualifications do not exactly match those specified by the employer, point this out in the letter and give evidence that you have the relevant experience to enable you handle the job.

• Information suggesting when you could be available for an interview, as well as how you can be contacted before then if need be.

In order to make the cover letter more appealing and effective, it should be neat in appearance, clear and polite in communication, and free of grammatical errors.

Paragraphs and Contents
First Paragraph

The first paragraph of the cover letter should be designed to capture the manager's attention and sustain his interest in reading further. You can achieve this by using any of the four attention grabbing techniques shown below:

1. By giving a brief summary of your specific qualifications that match the requirements for the job at hand. For example, you could start the letter by stating:

My diploma in secretarial studies and certificate in information technology qualify me for the Personal Assistant's position that you advertised in the Daily Nation on Monday the 15th of August.

2. By beginning your letter with reference to the company's latest developments, you come out as someone informed, interested in the company, and worth listening to. For example:

During a recent interview on KTN, Mr. Mwamburi, your CEO, outlined your company's strategy for seizing the emerging business opportunities in Southern Sudan and the wider East African region. Please consider my B. Com. degree with majors in marketing, and my two years' experience as a motor vehicle sales executive with Toyota East Africa, as you look for the best team to send to your new branches in these markets.

3. If you are writing in response to an advert or if you have been asked to send your credentials by someone personally

known to the human resource manager, you can immediately grab his attention by referring to any of these:

Example 1: writing in reference to an advert

I am sending this application in response to your advert appearing in The People Daily on Tuesday the 23rd of August, requiring Computer Networking Technicians.

Example 2: sending your application under somebody's instructions

Caution: Use this approach only when certain that the person you are talking about is personally known to the employment manager, and that the two are in good terms.

Mr. Andrew Kitsao of Family Bank has asked me to send you my credentials for consideration for a computer technician's job. He has informed me that you have such a position in your newly formed department of Information Technology, and that you could consider me for the position. My qualifications and experience match your requirements.

4. A fourth and more adventurous way of capturing the manager's attention is by asking a thought provoking question. This method is especially recommended for those sending unsolicited applications for it does a nice job at opening up communication.

Example 1

Does your theatre troupe require the services of a talented actress who can sing alto, play the solo guitar and act? Here I am.

Example 2

> *Does your school require the services of a Montessori trained nursery school teacher with three years of working experience? I am that person.*

Second Paragraph

In the second paragraph, build the manager's interest in your worth by first highlighting your qualifications and experience, and second, by inviting him to read the attached CV. This is also where you should market your strengths and express your eagerness to work for his organization.

Example 1: an ex-police officer wishing to join a private security firm

> *My rigorous training at Kiganjo Police Training College and my four years experience as a corporal serving in the North Easter and Nairobi provinces make me an asset worth your consideration. Should you hire me, I will gladly bring along a wealth of knowledge and experience in intelligence gathering for crime prevention, on-the-scene handling of crime, as well as investigation skills to guarantee your clients the security they so much need. Please see my attached Curriculum Vitae for more details.*

Example 2: a beautician

> *My intensive training at Garissa School of Beauty and Cosmetology, coupled with my three months' attachment at Linda's Beauty Palour in Moyale will enable me to offer services that will be to your clients' satisfaction. For more details on my qualifications please see the enclosed Curriculum Vitae.*

Third Paragraph

In the third or last paragraph, be specific and ask for an interview. After making this request, take control of the process and promise to call the manager in about a week's time to fix a date for the interview at his or her convenience. Also, give your contacts just in case the manager wishes to call you before then.

By promising to follow things up with a phone call to the manager, you reduce the chances of your application ending up in the receptionist's dust bin. In addition, you eliminate the 'waiting in the dark period' that falls between the moments you send the mail and when you receive response. Below are some good ways of ending a cover letter.

Example 1: a student who is about to complete college

May I have an interview? I will call your office next week with a view to arranging a convenient date and time. In case you wish to contact me before then, you may call my campus number (6899) 5875765757. After 12th of September, you can reach me on my home number (668) 6986986.

Thank you for your consideration.

Example 2: a general way of ending the letter

I would appreciate the opportunity to discuss how I can make a contribution to your company. I will call your office on the 10th of July so we can schedule an interview at your convenience. Should you wish to contact me before then, you may use the e-mail address above or call at (689) 696966.

Thank you for your consideration.

Signing Off

This is where you put your closing remarks such as Yours Faithfully, Sincerely, Truly, etc., and then your name. Remember to leave enough space for your signature between these words and your name. This section can be aligned either to the left, centre or to the right hand side of the page.

If you are sending the letter accompanying a copy of your CV, indicate this by writing: "Enc. Résumé" or "Enc. Curriculum Vitae." below your name.

Sample Cover Letters

Below are three sample cover letters. In the first one, the applicant is responding to a classified advert. The challenge is that she lacks the required academic background, but has some good working experience in the advertised field.

The second one is also a response to a classified advert whereby the applicant meets all the qualifications required by the employer, while the third and final one is an unsolicited application using the provoking question technique.

See how each of the letters has been designed to capture the manager's attention, create interest in the applicant's qualifications and capabilities, and how frankly they ask for an interview in the closing paragraphs.

Example 1: applicant lacking the required academic background but has some experience in the advertised field.

Christine Amunga Ababu

P.o Box 5578 – 6789

Migori.

24th July ____

To:

The Human Resource Manager

Taita Dairy Products

P.o Box 5557 – 557

Wundanyi.

Dear Mrs. Khadija Ahmed,

RE: APPLICATION FOR A FOOD TECHNOLOGIST'S POSITION

I am sending this application in response to your advertisement for the above named position, which appeared in the Standard on July 20, ___. My experience matches your requirements.

While you asked for a Bachelor's degree in Daily Technology, mine is a BSc. majoring in microbiology. However, I know that my three years of working experience at the New KCC in a capacity similar to your advertised position will be of great interest to you. Please see the enclosed Curriculum Vitae for more details.

I am looking forward to an opportunity to discuss how I can contribute to your company's progress. I will call you in the morning of Monday the 2nd to arrange an interview at your convenience. In the meantime, I may be reached at: (0786) 46456676 or crisamunga@getmail.com.

Thank you for your consideration.

Yours Truly,

Christine Amunga Ababu.

Enc. Curriculum Vitae.

Example 2: in response to a classified advert, whereby the applicant meets all the requirements set by the employer. He thus illustrates confidently how his skills and experience match the employer's stated requirements.

Simon Karanja Wanderi

P.o Box 5576-575

Namanga

8th -Jan __

To:

The Human Resource Manager

Dixons Products Limited

P.o Box 4364564-43534

Kitengela.

Dear Eng. Stephen Naimasia,

RE: APPLICATION FOR A SYSTEMS ANALYST'S POSITION

Kindly accept this as my application for the above named position, which was advertised in the January issue of the Small Medium Enterprises Today magazine. My qualifications and experience match your requirements as summarized below. For more details on this please see the attached Curriculum Vitae.

Your Requirements	My Qualifications
Database management skills	*Microsoft Access and Oracle*
Computer networking	*Windows NT and Cisco networking*

Web design	Visual Web Developer, DHTML and Dream Weaver
Two years experience	Two years experience
BSc. in computer science	BSc. in computer science

I welcome the opportunity to meet with you, at your convenience, to further discuss your needs and how I could work for you. I will call your office in the morning of 15th of January so we can arrange an interview. In the meantime, I may be contacted at (7678) 89678968.

Thank you for your consideration.

Yours Sincerely,

Simon Karanja Wanderi

Enc. résumé.

Example 3: an unsolicited letter of application using the provoking question technique.

Davis Musyoka Muli

P.o Box 6683 – 0867

Miritini.

19th – August 20__

To:

The Human Resource Manager

Sweets and Cakes Ltd.

P.o Box 56589 – 0987

Bahari.

Dear Mr. Manjit Patel,

RE: A HIGHLY MOTIVATED SALESMAN

Does your business require the services of a professionally trained and highly motivated salesman? Then here I am.

My diploma in sales and marketing from Kilifi Business Institute and my six months of working experience as an FMCG salesman with Kanji Agencies will enable me to greatly contribute towards the attainment of your sales targets. For more details on my qualifications and experience please see the enclosed résumé.

I look forward to meeting you soon to discuss how my skills and experience can boost your sales. I will call you next week on Friday so we can arrange an interview at your convenience. In the meantime, I may be reached at (567) 668688.

Thank you in advance.

Yours Faithfully,

Davis Musyoka Muli.

Enc. résumé.

5

Writing
an Effective CV

*"There is no passion to be found in playing small
– in settling for a life that is less than what you are
capable of living."*

- Nelson Mandela

Curriculum Vitae, also known as résumé, is a job search document that you send to prospective employers, giving them a preview of your skills, experience and abilities. The CV usually accompanies a cover letter in which you express interest in a vacancy.

Often, applicants put more emphasis in writing a compelling CV at the expense of the cover letter, something that works to their disadvantage. Just as you would experience revulsion if someone gave you a shoddy invitation to his home, likewise the manager feels when shoddily invited, in the cover letter, to read the CV.

Ideally, a CV is one of the strongest tools that you can use to market yourself to any prospective employer. This document should be crafted so as to serve the following three functions:

1. It should convince the prospective employer that you have what it takes to handle the job in question, and it would

therefore be worth their while talking to you in person in an interview.

The content of your CV should thus be tailored to marshal out your strengths that match the requirements set out by the employer. For instance, if the employer requires a Mathematics teacher with five years of working experience, this should be reflected in your CV. It is only by doing this that you can hope to arouse sufficient interest in the employer's mind to warrant his inviting you for an interview.

2. By giving details about your academic background and work experience, the CV acts as a guide to the interviewer when forming the questions to ask you in these areas.

For this purpose, the niceties that you include in the CV should be correct and verifiable. If possible, consider putting down only the facts for which you can produce documentary evidence if required to.

3. The CV serves as a permanent reference record that the employer can use whenever the need arises to compare your qualifications with those of your competitors. This is a common practice among managers when short listing who to call for the next round of interviews or when making the final decision on who to hire. Your CV should thus contain accurate facts that reflect your strengths and aptitude.

How are CVs evaluated?
Evaluation of CVs depends on the organization that you are sending your application to. In small organizations, the human resource manager could have the time to read through all documents and hopefully reply immediately. However, in big organizations that handle large volumes of correspondence, managers hardly ever get the time to read each CV from the first word to the last.

Most managers in such institutions mandate their deputies or secretaries to open the letters and check whether applicants have met the specifications set in the job advert. This forms the first elimination stage for those who fail to qualify.

Upon receiving the documents for qualified candidates, the manager races through the CV to find out what outstanding attributes a contender boasts above the cut off point. If the advert specifies that those with higher qualifications will have an added advantage, then these special cases are sorted out and set apart.

The manager then makes a short list of the most promising candidates out of all the applications received and invites them for an interview.

The general outlook of your CV is imperative as it is believed to be a reflection of its owner. A neat document is believed to represent an equally neat personality and the vice versa. Poorly prepared CVs are usually eliminated at the preliminaries without a second glance. Other factors that can lead to elimination of an otherwise well written CV include:

• Lack of adequate academic qualifications in the appropriate field.

• A very long or imprecise CV.

• The applicant having held too many positions with different employers within a short period of time - job hoping.

Parts and Contents of a CV
As we shall see later, there are three main CV formats or types: the chronological, functional, and chrono-functional or combined formats. Despite the difference in the layout of these formats, the parts and contents of a CV are basically similar and can be grouped into the following categories (not necessarily

in this order):

- The heading.

- Career goals and objectives.

- Educational background.

- Work experience.

- Personal information.

- Miscellaneous.

- References.

The Heading

This is the first part of the CV and perhaps the easiest to prepare. In this section you should include the following details:

- Your full name.

- Contact address.

- Telephone number.

- E-mail address.

Once these have been put together, they form of a heading such as the one shown below:

Jane Atieno Okoth
P.o Box 67676-00200
Nairobi – city square
Tel: 0852 – 566464
E-mail:jakoth@network.com

Career Goals and Objectives

Career goals and objectives can be divided into immediate and long term intentions. Immediate objectives should be oriented towards acquiring the position at hand, while long term ones should be a reflection of your aspirations as you grow in your career.

Ideally, this is a very common part in the chronological format and comes after the heading. This also forms the first details section of the CV that the manager reads. From this section, he can tell right away whether your objectives are in line with those of the position available.

Besides ensuring that your goals reflect what the employer needs, you should also make sure that they are realistic and consistent with the qualifications and experience that you include in the later parts of the CV. For instance, a fresh college graduate with no prior working experience, but who puts his immediate career goal as capturing the CEO position in a multinational corporation is not likely to be taken seriously, given his minimal qualifications and lack of experience in management.

Different people develop their career goals and objectives in different ways, and here is one of them in five easy steps:

1. Put down your profession followed by your area of specialization. For example:

Counselling – marriage and family life.

2. Find out the level at which you will be joining the organization. This could be at the junior, middle or senior level, depending on the job advertisement. Modify your statement appropriately, eg:

Junior counsellor, marriage and family life.

3. Now that you have developed an idea of your immediate

career objective, compile the statement to show that your interest is in working with an organization such as the one run by your prospective employer. This could read as follows:

Immediate objective: *junior level marriage and family life counsellor with a non-governmental organization (NGO).*

4. To develop your long-term objectives statement, think of what you would like to be doing in your career, say, in ten years time. Now make a statement capturing that vision and put it down as your long-term career objective, e.g.:

Long-term objective: *progression to a senior marriage and family life consultant with a non-governmental organization (NGO).*

5. Finally, bring these statements together under the career goals and objectives heading as shown below:

Career goals and objectives

Immediate objective: *Entry level marriage and family life counsellor with a non-governmental organization (NGO).*

Long-term objective: *progression to a senior marriage and family life consultant with a non-governmental organization (NGO).*

Educational Background
In this section, put down the following information concerning your academic life:

- Your degree, diploma or certificate.

- Area of specialization.

• Institutions where you obtained your certificates.

• The year when you graduated from each institution.

• Order of merit, for example first class honours, credit, distinction, etc, with which you qualified.

Begin this section by listing your highest level of education. With good career training, details about your high school become less significant. Instead, incorporate particulars of any relevant projects you may have undertaken, your attachment, as well as any awards that you may have received in college. This is crucial if you do not have any working experience.

Develop this section well. Go beyond mere statement of facts that you undertook a project and show how that enabled you to acquire or sharpen a skill that the employer wants. For example, rather than simply saying:

Conducted a marketing survey in May, 2007.

You could add more relevance to the statement by giving further elaboration such as:

May, 2007 - Combined research and report writing skills in a marketing survey that sought to determine the effects of commodity packaging on consumers' purchasing behaviour.

In order to make your statements more compelling, begin each one of them with a verb – an action word – as in the above example. If you have a solid working history, then the work experience section that follows will be of more significance to you than educational background.

Work Experience
Most human resource managers believe that the easiest way

to tell an applicant's future performance is by reviewing his or her records of past accomplishments and failures. The work experience section of your CV gains significance before to the manager because he can tell the kind of person you are by reading your work history.

You should therefore endeavour to present yourself in a way that leaves no doubt about how effective you have been in your previous work stations. It is only in this way that you can convince the manager that by hiring you, he will be adding value to the organisation.

The details to include and the general organization of this section will largely depend on the CV format that you choose. Should you opt for the chronological format, you will begin by putting down your most recent job, then the second most recent, and worked backward in that order. Repeat this for each of the positions that you have previously held. A sample of this section in the chronological format is shown below:

Work experience

Employment dates	*20_ to date*
Employer	*Ministry of Agriculture*
Job title	*Field Extension Officer*
Job description	*Planning and coordination of farm demonstration activities in training farmers on the latest farming techniques*
Major achievements	*Taught farmers in my division effective farming techniques that saw their farm productivity increase by 60% in two years*

If using the functional format, you could group your experience according to skills and accomplishments, and then present them in the summary section of the CV as shown below:

Summary

Experience in administration of rural development projects, coordination of emergency relief operations, and conflict resolution.

If using the chrono – function format, you can blend the two approaches above to come up with a section such as:

Experience

Coast Institute of Leadership

Lecturer, 20_ to date

• *Assisting learners to develop effective leadership skills*

• *Teaching on the concept of power*

• *Teaching on the various leadership styles*

Personal Information

Many applicants include a number of not-so-relevant items in the personal information section of the CV, and so end up with an excessively long document.

Considering that your CV isn't your biography but a preview of your skills and abilities, the tips below should help you determine what to include and what to omit from this section.

• Include only the details you are certain will be of interest to the specific employer that you want to send the document to. For example, if he requires that you indicate your nationality, you can do so in this section.

• You don't have to include a picture of yourself.

• Do not include your religion, physical or health conditions unless you have been asked to. Assume the organisation is an equal opportunity employer.

• If you don't want to attract much attention to your age, put down your year of birth only, for example, 1982, and let the manager do the calculations if your age is that important to him.

• Regarding marital status, you can do without putting down the number of your children or dependents. Also, if a married woman and the job involves a lot of travelling, disclosing your marital status this early could put you at a disadvantage compared to your single competitors who might not have as much domestic restrictions.

In short, consider the possible effects – both positive and negative – before including any of the above or other personal details in the CV.

Miscellaneous

You can include other special sections in your CV in order to emphasize your all round personality. Such sections can come in a variety of titles such as:

• Hobbies and special interests.

• Professional affiliations.

• Student organizations and activities.

• Publications.

• Patents.

• Related achievements.

• Honours and awards.

Here, just like in all other sections above, include only the information you are sure will be of interest to the employer. For example, if you know that the company has a bias towards a certain sport – Kenya Pipeline and Kenya Commercial Bank are famous for women's volley ball, Telkom for women's hockey, while East African Breweries is known for men football – pointing out that you indeed participate in such activities could turn out interesting to the employer.

References/Referees
In this section, put down names and contact details of at least three people whom the employer can contact if he wishes to find out more about you. Such should be people familiar with you, and should be able to comment objectively about you.

Good references could include your former employers, college or university lecturers, your pastor or priest and former classmates in respectable positions. Ideally, you should not include your relatives as referees as they are likely to be biased. Before compiling your list of references, contact all the persons you wish to include and informed them of your intentions.

This section is nonetheless not a mandatory one, so if you feel that including it could make your CV too long, you can leave it out and instead write: "Reference available on request." Should you wish to include the references on a page of their own, be sure to indicate: "References attached" at the bottom of your last details page, then label the attached page containing the references appropriately, e.g.: "References for Jane Atieno Okoth."

Length of the CV
For people with less than ten years of working experience, a CV that is a page or two in length is sufficient. Those with a

long trail of publications or with above ten years of working experience with different employers and in positions relevant to the one at hand can take in a third page or so.

A very long CV is seen as lacking in brevity, which is a sign of unpolished communication skills. Bear the following in mind as you prepare this crucial document:

• As you progress in your career life, your level of experience will continue to grow, and so the work experience section of your CV will gain more significance over the other section. This will necessitate that you keep editing your CV to capture these new changes.

• Each employer wants to be regarded as important in his own rights, so poorly prepared application documents are almost always given poor consideration by human resource managers.

• Edit your CV carefully to make sure that it is free of grammatical mistakes.

• When printing your CV, you don't have to use expensive or coloured paper unless you are an artist or a designer. Instead, use the standard A4 size white paper that is commonly used for most document preparation works.

• Store your CV in a CD or any other digital storage medium for easy editing as need arise.

6

CV Formats

"Vigilance in watching opportunity; tact and daring in seizing upon opportunity; force and persistence in crowding opportunity to its utmost of possible achievement—these are the martial virtues which must command success." —Austin Phelps

There are three general CV formats:

1. The chronological.

2. The functional.

3. The chrono – functional or combined format.

Each of the above formats emphasizes a different aspect of you as briefly discussed below. The next chapter is designed to deepen your understanding of how different challenges such as ill health, physical disability and inadequate qualifications can be overcome using the different CV formats. For now, we will only introduce the formats and a sample of each.

The Chronological Format
This is the darling of most fresh graduates. Here, information on the applicant's educational background, being perhaps the strongest achievement that one has so far, is presented first, beginning with the highest level to the lowest. Work experience – including attachments - is also presented beginning with the most recent and going back in time. This is also the best format

for those who have had an uninterrupted academic or working life.

Example of a chronological CV for someone with work experience

Andrew Kosgey Cheruiyot

P.o Box 55776 – 668

Nakuru.

Tel: (6889) 567-6654

Career Goals and Objectives

To secure a job as Senior Fleet Manager with Excel Logistics.

Experience

Employment dates	20_ to date
Employer	National Cereals and Produce Board (NCPB), Nakuru branch
Job title	Assistant Transport Manager
Key responsibilities	i) Preparation of monthly budgets for the transport department
	ii) Preparation of weekly work schedule for drivers, loaders and mechanics
	iii) Ensuring that the Board's vehicles are in running condition
Achievements	Reduced the transport department's annual operations cost by 20% in one year
Employment dates	20_ to 20_

Employer	Maringo Transporters
Job title	Assistant Fleet Manager
Key responsibilities	i) Efficiency monitoring
	ii) Preparation of the department's procurement documents
Achievements	Ensured efficient running of a fleet of 70 heavy commercial trucks and a staff of 150 drivers, loaders and mechanics

Educational Background

Dates	199_ to 20__
Institution	Kenya Polytechnic
Course	HND. Mechanical Engineering
Specialization	Automotive Engineering
Order of merit	Credit
Dates	199_ to 199_
Institution	Eldoret Polytechnic
Course	Dip. Mechanical Engineering
Specialization	Automotive Engineering
Order of merit	Credit

Personal Details

Date of birth	197_
Marital status	Married
Nationality	Kenyan

Hobbies and other Interests

Volleyball and swimming

References

Dr. Andrew Kinoti

University of Nairobi

P.o Box 30197

Nairobi.

Tel: (799) 5756757.

Purity Mwanzia

P.o Box 56765

Amukula.

Tel: (657) 76575.

David Mwadime

P.o Box 46347 – 5665

Mombasa.

Tel: (765) 567567.

The Functional Format

This is the format most commonly used by those making career changes or people who have had interruption gaps in their academic or working lives. The format lets you emphasize what you can do as opposed to what you have already done.

Work experience details are grouped according to skills rather than according to employers, date and achievements order used in the chronological format.

Example of Functional CV

Andrew Kosgey Cheruiyot

P.o Box 55776 – 668

Nakuru

Tel: (7868) 654645

Summary

Experience in fleet management with proven abilities in:

- Budget preparation

- Efficiency monitoring

- Work scheduling

- Motor vehicle maintenance

Areas of Competence

Management: work scheduling skills to ensure transport budget remains within projected limits.

Efficiency Monitoring: ensuring optimum use of manpower and machine.

Experience

Assistant transport manager, National Cereals and Produce Board (NCPB)

(20_ to date)

Assistant fleet manager, Maringo transporters

(20_ to 20_)

Personal Details

Date of birth	197_
Marital status	Married
Nationality	Kenyan

Hobbies and other Interests

Volleyball and swimming

References

Dr. Andrew Kinoti

University of Nairobi

P.o Box 30197

Nairobi.

Tel: (799) 5756757.

Purity Mwanzia

P.o Box 56765

Amukula.

Tel: (657) 76575.

David Mwadime

P.o Box 46347 – 5665

Mombasa.

Tel: (765) 567567.

The Chrono-Functional or Combined Format
This format combines some aspects of both the chronological and functional formats, and is commonly used by applicants with only a little working experience. Since it contains some elements of the functional format, it can also be used by people with career gaps or those changing from one career to another.

Just like in the chronological format, academic and work experience details are presented beginning with the most recent and going back in time.

Example of a chrono-functional or combined CV:

Andrew Kosgey Cheruiyot

P.o Box 55776 – 668

Nakuru

Tel: (7868) 654645

Career goals and objectives

To secure a job as Senior Fleet Manager with Excel Logistics.

Qualifications

Management: work scheduling skills to ensure prompt delivery of goods so as to meet deadlines set by customers.

Budget and efficiency monitoring: effective budget preparation and efficiency monitoring to ensure transport budget remains within the projected limits, while maintaining optimum use of manpower and machine.

Experience

National Cereals and Produced Board (NCPB)

Assistant transport manager 20_ to date

- Preparation of monthly budget for the Board's transport department

- Preparation of weekly work schedules for drivers, loaders and mechanics

- Ensuring the Board's vehicles are in running condition

Marigo Transporters

Assistant fleet manager   20_ to 20_

- Efficiency monitoring

- Preparation of the department's procurement documents

Education

Kenya polytechnic   **199_ to 20_**

HND. Mechanical engineering –Automotive

Eldoret polytechnic   **199_ to 19_**

Dip. Mechanical engineering – Automotive

Personal details

Date of birth   197_

Marital status   Married

Nationality   Kenyan

Hobbies and other interests

Volleyball and swimming

References

Dr. Andrew Kinoti

University of Nairobi

P.o Box 30197

Nairobi.

Tel: (799) 5756757.

Purity Mwanzia

P.o Box 56765

Amukula.

Tel: (657) 76575.

David Mwadime

P.o Box 46347 – 5665

Mombasa.

Tel: (765) 567567.

7

Overcoming the Hurdles

"Nothing in the world can take the place of persistence. Talent will not; nothing is more common than unsuccessful men with talent. Genius will not; unrewarded genius is almost a proverb. Education will not; the world is full of educated derelicts. Persistence and determination alone are omnipotent. The slogan, 'press on,' has solved and always will solve the problems of the human race."

- Calvin Coolidge

Approaching an employer and succeeding in making him take you in and leave out other contenders requires a tough strategy. This is more so if you fall short of the requirements stated by the employer in the advert, yet you strongly feel that this is the job for you.

Some of the challenges that we will learn how to circumvent in this chapter include: inadequate academic qualifications, lack of enough job experience, job hoping, ill health, disability, and HIV/AIDS.

In these and a number of similar cases, the key to meeting the employer lies in withholding information on your inadequacies during the initial elimination stages and making the disclosure later on during the interview, or when you can best defend your condition.

Alternatively, you can make the disclosure early, but do so in such a subtle way that the employer gets convinced that the condition is not likely to interfere with your productivity in any adverse way.

1. Inadequate Work Experience

This can be the case when you either lack the required number of working years or when your experience happens to be in a different field. Inadequate experience can be a major challenge for both fresh graduates and experienced employees seeking to change careers. The assumption in the minds of most human resource managers is that novices might take a long time to learn the ropes, and are likely to make mistakes that could turn out expensive for the company.

On the other hand, it is assumed that experienced applicants will settle down immediately to work and start contributing to the company's productivity, hence the emphasis on adequate experience on the job.

Sadly, these assumptions overlook the fact that some of the applicants with little or no previous work experience, but who are rich in technical training and are raving to launch their careers, often get on the job and outperform their experienced counterparts.

There are at least three methods of getting around this challenge and increasing your chances of being invited for the interview:

• *Getting acquainted with the human resource manager*. A simple way of achieving this is by getting one of his many trusted friends to introduce you to him either formally or informally. This can give you the opportunity you need to explain to the manager your situation and demonstrate your desire to take on the job.

• In the event that it becomes impossible to get acquainted with the manager, then *explain your situation to him or her using the cover letter that you send with your CV*. In this way, you can clarify that although you lack the required number of working years, you can take up the job and do it satisfactorily.

• The third method can be used either on its own or in combination with any of the two above. When designing your CV, use the functional format and modify it as follows:

a) Omit the summary section and instead put an alternative statement describing your job searching objective. For example:

Career objectives: *junior level counselor, marriage and family life.*

b) Instead of major accomplishments, write your own section titled *key qualifications* or any other suitable title to draw the manager's attention from your inexperience to the abundance of your skills. For example:

Key Qualifications

Script writing *– excellent skills in script writing for plays and documentaries.*

Audio-visual editing *– excellent skills in the use of Adobe premiere and Pinnacle Studio for digital motion picture, as well as Adobe Audition, Cubase and Sound Forge for professional audio production.*

2. Inadequate Academic Qualifications

This situation can take at least three different forms:

• When the employer wants, say, a degree in Business Administration, but you only have a diploma supported by a few years of working experience.

• The employer wants the above named degree, but yours happens to be in Commerce or Economics.

• You have a new diploma or degree that most employers in the market seem not familiar with.

When confronted with thousands of applications from candidates with the above three or more conditions, employers resort to the law of supply and demand, and academic qualifications as stipulated by the employer become a key consideration. Getting the right candidate becomes a negative screening process, whereby those who fail to meet the prescribed qualifications are left out of the short list.

On the other hand, when the company badly needs a certain skill yet only a handful of candidates apply for the position, experience rather than academics, becomes the determining factor. Given this, and irrespective of your shortcomings in academic qualifications, you can still convince the employer that you are the best candidate for the job.

You can reserve your voucher to the interview by using your CV to draw evidence from your past performance on similar jobs. You can rely on the functional format here, as it gives you an opportunity to put your achievements and capabilities before your academic history.

Achievements and capabilities being your strongest selling points, make the sections dealing with these more detailed in order to give a better illustration of what you can do. In addition, if you have a diploma or degree that you sense the employer could find unfamiliar, consider giving a brief description of it or giving its known equivalent already in the market. For instance:

B.A. Government (Political science and public administration) or Dip. Social work (related to sociology)

3. Job Hopping

This refers to having worked for many employers within a short span of time. If you didn't know, this is a negative trait as it points out to one's unreliability.

Different professions have varying levels of what they consider as acceptable job hoping. For instance, most project based jobs, especially in the construction industry, are prone to job hoping since for every assignment that ends with one contractor, another begins elsewhere with a different company. Most employers understand this and so make their decisions based on what they consider as reasonable levels of job hoping in their specific fields.

To be on the safe side, consider putting down just a few of your previous employers though you might have had good reasons for moving from one employer to another. Alternatively, should you choose to include all positions, give reasons why you left them. Some of the acceptable reasons for moving on that you could include in your CV are:

- *Mergers and acquisitions* – if your previous company merged with, or was bought out by another and your position was scraped off or taken over by an employee from the other company.

- *Nepotism* – if your position was taken over by a relative of the proprietor.

• *Industrial restructuring* – if as a result of some changes at your previous company your position was either eliminated or its budgetary allocation slashed badly thus making it difficult for you to operate. An alternative of this is if your functions were merged with those of another department.

• *Lack of opportunities for advancement* – if you realized that you were using only a few of your skills and there seemed to be no opportunities for your personal and career development.

• *Health* – if the condition of your personal health or that of a person under your care made it difficult for you to continue working in your previous environments.

When using this as a reason, take care not to portray yourself as a weakling, as this can put you at a disadvantage. Instead, show evidence that the situation will not affect your productivity at work.

Some of the unacceptable reasons for leaving your previous employer include:

• Chronic absenteeism that got you sacked.

• Fighting, alcoholism and drug abuse.

• Serious marital or other problems that may have adversely interfered with your performance at work.

• Theft, or incompatibility with your previous managers, supervisors or work mates, among other reasons.

Create an honest list of all your previous jobs, employers and reasons for leaving. See which ones among them are worthy listing in your CV and which ones are not. The functional CV format comes in handy at this juncture, as it allows you to put your accomplishments before your employment history. In so doing, you create an initial positive image of yourself, one that makes up for any shortcomings there might be in your employment records. Also, screen out any bad records from your CV and leave only those that show you in positive light as an achiever.

If you opt for the chronological format, you can include a brief reason for your departure from an employer after the achievements section. Remember to include only reasons that are acceptable as shown below:

Employment dates	20_ to 20_
Employer	Kanji and Kanji contractors
Job title	Project manager
Job description	Project design, budgeting and supervision.
Major achievements	Implemented efficient management techniques that brought down the cost of major projects by 15%
Reason for leaving	Winding up of the company

4. Disability or ill Health
Being physically challenged or suffering from health conditions such as HIV/AIDS, cancer, asthma, heart attack, and mental problems can limit one's chances of securing a job in some organisations. One of the major reasons why some managers tend to discriminate against applicants with complicated health conditions is the fear that such people might not be

able to withstand the pressure to perform. In most cases, section managers' promotion and salary increments are based on their units' productivity, hence the concern that hiring an ill or physically challenged person would be to their own disadvantage.

Modern human resource managers understand that health challenges can happen to anyone, themselves included, and that the law prohibits discriminations in recruitment of staff. Second, it is faulty reasoning to equate disability to inability. Given the opportunity, most of the skilled but handicapped or ill individuals can work as productively if not better than their healthy counterparts.

If you are not sure whether your prospective employer is an equal opportunity organisation, avoid mentioning anything about your condition until you meet at the interview. In cases when the employer states that preference will be given to those with conditions similar to yours, or should you find it necessary to inform the employer of your condition for any other reason, it is advisable to do it in the cover letter rather than in the CV.

When doing this, bear in mind that the employer's principal concern is your skills, and this is what should come first in the letter. Afterwards, you can give a brief and honest description of your condition with the aim of showing that it won't interfere with your productivity. Such a description could go as follows:

Three years ago I was diagnosed as being HIV positive. I immediately went for anti – retroviral treatment (ART), and I have since then been able to live a positive and productive career life. This can be attested to by my recent promotion from a sales representative to the assistant marketing manager at Kangemi Plastic Manufacturing Limited...

5. Age

Most companies shop for management trainees from the cadres of fresh graduates within the 23 – 27 age brackets. Besides being sharp minded, people within these ages are considered as being in their formative stage career-wise, and can be easily moulded to fit into the corporate culture.

As they approach age 30, it is argued that most people have developed stability of character and good decision-making skills which are required for middle level to senior management positions.

An applicant's age becomes an issue when the employer stipulates the required limits for a given post, while the applicant has either not attained, or has exceeded the set limits. Age can also become a bigger issue for applicants above 40 but seeking junior positions. Things can get even more complicated for women, who are by that age considered as being beyond their 'creative' period.

If only a slight difference of say, a year, exists between your age and the required limit, this might not be a big issue so long as you have fulfilled all the other requirements. But should the difference get wider than this, the situation requires a stealthy approach to overcome.

One way of doing this is by honestly disclosing the fact to the employer in the cover letter. When doing this, once again begin by marshalling out your strongest achievements and qualifications. After you have created a favourable impression of yourself in the manager's mind, mention the age factor and show evidence from your previous successes that the difference in age won't interfere with your performance in any way.

In case you have surpassed the age limit by a wide margin, you can edit your CV in the following ways to draw attention away from your age:

• Omit your age or date of birth details from the personal section.

• Scan the entire document to ensure that nothing gives clue of your age. You can achieve this by, for example, leaving out information concerning jobs you held long time ago or by leaving out the dates when you completed school. The justification for doing this is that the CV gives only a summary of your achievements and potentials, which is different from your autobiography.

Chapter

8

Preparing
For the Interview

*"There is a powerful driving force inside every human
being that once unleashed can make any vision, or
desire a reality."*

- Anthony Robbins

An interview is a formal meeting where you will be asked some questions in order to gauge your suitability for the position that you applied for. Such a meeting can take place at the human resource manager's office, at the company's boardroom or at any other convenient place.

An interview can be conducted by a single or a panel of interviewers from the company or a recruitment agency. In some cases and depending on the job, the interview can turn informal and be conducted outside the boardroom. This happens especially when you are being evaluated on technical skills such as driving and machine operation.

In all this, the employer's chief concern in you can be summarized as follows:

• Your attitude towards yourself, the employer and towards others.

• Your skills and experience, and how they have prepared you to add value to the organisation.

• How soon you can adapt to the system and start contributing to the organisation's productivity.

• Your salary requirements.

When preparing for the interview you need to polish up in the following areas too: physical appearance, expression of courtesy, ability to communicate effectively, use of common sense, and demonstration of self-confidence.

Receiving invitation to an interview is sure evidence that you've already impressed the employer. What you need to do now is prove that what he thinks of you is right.

You can exceed the interviewer's expectations by conducting further research in the following areas: the company's directors and the entire top brass, the company's range of products, their customers, as well as major competitors in the market.

Matching Your Skills with Job Requirements

Find out too, all you can about the requirements for the job you will be interviewing for. Where possible, request the company to mail you the job description and key responsibilities.

With this, begin matching every requirement for the job with your skills. For instance, if the job requires competence in information technology with special emphasis on database management and web design, you could indicate, on a draft piece of paper, that you have already trained in MS Access and Dream Weaver respectively.

Of course, there will be areas in which you might not be as strong as you are required to, but this shouldn't worry you so long as you can show how your other skills make up for the short coming and demonstrate willingness to learn what you don't know already.

For instance, if there is requirement for a valid driving license which you don't have, you can convince the employer that you wouldn't mind working as a team with others who already have the licence as you make plan to get your own. You will be surprised that most employers put attitude before skills, and so long as you show a forward inclined way of thinking, you can easily make up for any shortfalls in your weaker areas.

Physical Appearance

Most interviewers reason that if you don't care much about yourself, you probably won't care about the job. For this reason, the first impression that you create of yourself, usually determined by your dressing and level of self-confidence, will greatly determine whether you get the job or not.

It's true that there is a relationship between how you dress and your level of self-confidence. When you are certain that you look attractive and professional, you exude more confidence, and the vice versa.

As a basic dressing principal, women should wear clothes that fit well; with matching colours, a pair of low – heeled shoes, and without excessive or noisy jewellery. Men should also adorn well fitting clothes.

The shirt should especially fit well at the collar, now that they may have to wear a necktie. Dark or gray coloured suits with matching long sleeved shirts, and a well polished pair of black or brown shoes look great.

If the job advert doesn't mention anything to do with religion, avoid carrying along items such as rosaries, crucifixes, rings or literature that could indicate your faith.

Arrange the Portfolio

In your preparation for the interview make sure that you pack the following in your folder:

- The letter inviting you to the interview.

- Reference notes indicating job description, core competencies required, as well as questions you might need to ask the interviewer.

- Original identity card or passport.

- Originals of all of your certificates.

- Original testimonials – recommendation letters, etc.

- A writing pad and pen.

- Any other item the interviewer may have asked for in the letter inviting you to the interview.

In case you have to reproduce some copies of your documents, do so at least a day before the interview. Also, to avoid the unpleasant surprise of discovering too late that you have misplaced important documents, cross check to ascertain that everything is okay at least a day before the interview.

Rehearse

If geniuses can afford the time to run ideas through their minds before making a presentation, why not you? Take some quiet moments and visualize the interview.

Picture yourself already before the panel and listen to them firing questions at you. What is it they are asking that you haven't prepared to handle yet? You can also get a friend to help you in simulating the interview. See Appendix B for some of the frequently asked interview questions.

9

The Interview

*"There comes that mysterious meeting in our life
when someone acknowledges who we are and
what we can be, igniting the circuits of our highest
potential." - Rusty Berkus*

At the Company

Arrive early for the interview. Ensure that your phone is either off or in vibration mode, and that your shoes are well polished. Then, relax and ask the receptionist for the most recent issue of the company's newsletter. You can also read the notice board to see whether there is anything related to the interview. Generally, familiarise yourself with the company's environment.

Inside the Interview Room

Once invited into the interview room, enter confidently but also with a show of courtesy. Do not hesitate at the door. Wait to be shown where to sit, and if offered a handshake, respond with a firm one.

Once seated, assume an alert and confident posture, avoiding the temptation to sink deeper into the seat.

Although it is natural to experience a mild degree of nervousness, take control of your feelings and know that the interviewer will also be trying to make you feel comfortable before anything serious begins.

Some of the common signs of nervousness that you should avoid by all means include: hesitating to answer simple and direct questions, especially those relating to your identity; cracking your knuckles; biting of lips; sneaking glances at your watch or the wall clock; as well as beginning your responses with a sigh or expressions such as: "Oh my God!, My goodness!" etc.

Listen carefully as the chief interviewer introduces the rest of the panel to you. Take down each interviewer's name and position in the company for two good reasons:

1. Responding to each interviewer by name brings you out as an intelligent person. Be careful though, not to mix up the names as it can be embarrassing.

2. You will need these names and positions when doing follow up after the interview.

Handling the Quick Fire
Once the interview is underway, be alert. For every question posed to you, no matter how simple it might sound, resist the temptation to fire an answer back. Instead:

• Ensure that you have heard the question right. If not, ask the interviewer to kindly repeat.

• Ensure that you understand what the question is leading to and whether it contains any tricks or hidden implications.

• When responding to questions, draw illustrations from your academic or work experience to support your answer.

• Speak clearly, and use appropriate gestures.

• Cover sufficiently all the areas of interest that each question touches on.

• Maintain sufficient levels of eye contact with each of the interviewers. Looking someone straight in the eyes shows boldness on your part. By observing the interviewer's body movements and gestures, you can tell with ease what is at the back of his mind.

• No matter how interesting the encounter turns out to be, resist the temptation to talk too much.

Essential qualities such as intelligence, power of decision making, as well as your ethical standards will be evaluated from how you respond to various types of questions.

As much as you can, maintain an optimistic outlook during the entire session. Do not panic even when asked a question whose answer you might not readily have, neither should you present false information. Instead, admit that you would need some time to find an appropriate reply to such a question. In so doing, you boost your counts on honesty.

Most of the questions that interviewers ask require elaboration. This means you should guard against giving monosyllabic answers such as "Yes" or "No" on the one hand, and against talking too much on the other. When giving elaboration, go directly to the point and give a few relevant illustrations from your experience, and that's all.

No Arguments!
Never start an argument with interviewers. Should you find yourself in a position whereby your point of view differs significantly from that of the panellists, start by accepting their point of view as the right one. Then, using an appropriate transitional word or connector of contrast such as: *however,*

nonetheless, on the other hand, etc. introduce your point of view as just another viable suggestion. Even should you feel that the interviewers' point of view is out rightly wrong, do not be adamant about it, neither should you insist that yours is the absolute right one.

In case a question comes regarding your previous employer, resist the temptation to paint a pessimistic impression of him, no matter how terrible he might have been to you. Bitterness and negative criticism can portray you as a difficult person to deal with. You don't want to be seen from this perspective.

Four Major Stages of an Interview
A typical interview consists of four main stages:

- The opening or introduction

- The interviewer's questions session

- The interviewee's questions session

- The end or closing

Assuming that our typical interview lasts for thirty minutes, each of the above stages could last for a period of time as shown in the discussion below:

1. The Opening
This lasts for between one and five minutes from the moment you enter the interview room. During this period, the interviewer welcomes you and asks general questions about yourself. This is also when he will introduce the rest of the panel to you.

Besides trying to make you feel at ease, the interviewer will be evaluating you on the lines of maturity of character, self – confidence, level of enthusiasm in the job, as well as on your communication skills. This is also when he will ask for your original certificates and other testimonials that you might have carried along. Most likely, he will have, on the table, a file containing the cover letter and CV that you send when applying for the job.

In short, this is a very important phase in the quest for you dream job since this is when the interviewer forms his first impressions of you. To win him over, be your best!

2. The Interviewer's Questions

This is the second and often the longest of all sessions, taking anything from five to fifteen minutes. Questions in this section focus on the following core areas: your achievements; work experience and specialised skills; as well as your level of understanding of the job and potential for career growth.

Here, the interviewer wants to see how your performance in these areas qualifies you for the job for which you are interviewing. In order to maximize your chances of getting the job, you need to prepare yourself for this section in two ways:

1. By thoroughly understanding the needs of the employer and the skills required for that job.

2. By understanding your self-worth: the expertise you are selling to the company.

By understanding the specific needs that the employer intends to fulfil, you can tailor your presentation to meet those needs. In other words, you will know where you need to kick the ball in order to score. No wild shots!

Assessing your self-worth in terms of skills, knowledge and achievements can be tricky for some people, mainly due to their tendency to either exaggerate or underrate themselves. However, you can achieve some degree of objectivity by outlining, on a piece of paper, all your areas of training, key achievements and skills, and how they relate to the job at hand.

Once again, bear in mind that with every question that the interviewer asks, he wants you to open up and say more. For example, when he asks you: "Can you briefly tell us something about your previous job?"

You can start by briefly giving its title, and then proceed to describe what your major responsibilities were, and finally, give an outstanding achievement that you had. Such a response could go as follows:

"My previous job was a graphics designer working with Mawazo publishers. I was responsible for the design of covers and illustrations in most of the publications that were done by the company for the four years that I worked there. Besides, I won the prize for designing the company's new logo, which captures the company's working philosophy and emphasis on customer satisfaction."

The above response contains the three cardinal ingredients:

Job title: Graphics designer with Mawazo publishers.

Responsibilities: Designing of covers and other illustrations for the books published by the company.

Achievements: Won the prize for designing the company's new logo.

Some interviewers are experts at asking the kind of questions that you would least expect. These are aimed at assessing how well you react to surprises or crises. Such questions might also be used to gauge your analytical skills and power of decision making.

For instance, you might be asked: "If you were to choose between being a cheetah and an ostrich, which one would you rather be and why?"

At first you might wonder why a cheetah or an ostrich of all wild animals? But in order to answer this satisfactorily, you need to know something beyond the basic fact that both are fast runners. You need to know that while the cheetah runs straight towards its target, an ostrich runs round and round in circles.

There are many other factors that you could consider when forming your response to such general knowledge questions. Nevertheless, ensure that whatever you say relates to your personal traits, abilities and skills, and how they relate to the job at hand.

As a winding up point, do not exaggerate your achievements, neither should you present forged documents as these can be verified online nowadays. Attempting to bribe an interviewer or requesting special favours is unacceptable too.

3. Interviewee's Questions

After the interviewer is through with his queries, a time comes for you to ask any questions you may wish to. This brief session lasts for approximately five minutes. Ideally, ask only a few intelligent questions regarding the company and the job, such as the following:

• What are some of the major challenges that I am likely to face while working with you?

• What is the company's policy as far as promotions are concerned?

• How will the company evaluate my performance on the job?

• What incentives exist to motivate the company's staff?

• Does the company have any form of orientation or training for new employees?

• How does the company work in order to beat its competitors in the market?

Quoting Your Preferred Salary

If there are more rounds of interviews expected, the question of salary may be discussed at an advanced stage if you qualify. But if there is only a single interview from which the best candidate will be picked, you can inquire about the pay package if the interviewer doesn't bring up the issue. Money matters are not only important, but sensitive too, and how you intend to handle this question should be guided by a number of factors that you're supposed to have researched in advance. These include:

a) The company's own salary package and allowances for your type of job and level of experience. Different employers give different amounts of salary and benefit packages for similar positions and qualifications. Proper understanding of your prospective employer's package or starting salary for new employees at your level of entry can therefore help you to come up with a realistic salary quotation.

b) If the position for which you're interviewing did not previously exist in the company, you can use this to support your salary quotation. You know they require someone competent enough to establish, say, a new department, and this might bring about roles and duties that were not previously envisaged in your job description.

c) If you are fresh from college and you have no previous work experience, asking for a high salary at this point might prove detrimental. You certainly need a place where you can start working and gain experience, after which you will climb to your dream position and earn your dream salary. Until then, show willingness to start where the corporate ladder starts for you.

d) If the company is interested in you chiefly because of your outstanding performance at your previous station, then they must be ready to pay you better than your previous employer.

In this case, quote a figure that is higher than your previous salary, but one that from your research, you know is within affordable range for the new organisation. Making yourself too expensive or too cheap can discourage some prospective employers from taking you.

e) The terms of employment, whether casual, temporary, part time, contract or permanent can also determine your salary quotation.

For most casual jobs, the company sets a fixed rate of pay per day depending on the nature of work and level of skill required. This is usually due to the abundant supply of labour and limited availability of job opportunities in the market.

f) In case you are seeking a job after losing a previous one, your financial obligations such as family upkeep and health care can dictate what you would consider as acceptable amount of pay. Depending on your luck, you could find yourself interviewing for a position paying a higher salary, or the vice versa.

In all this, the aim should be to enable you and the employer work out a remuneration package that is fair to the two of you.

If you do not succeed in getting the exact amount you initially hoped for, you can agree on a salary review to come after you have settled on the job.

Other questions that you could ask regarding salary include deductions such as Income Tax, contributions to the NSSF, NHIF and HELB as they may apply to you.

In ending your questions session, make the interviewer open up and tell you something about him or herself. By revealing something personal and positive, the two of you take the first step towards establishing a bond of mutual understanding. This also shows that you have a genuine concern for others, which creates a good impression of you. You can achieve this by posing a question such as: "What do you like most about your job?"

4. Closing

Gradually, discussions will move towards a natural end. This is the closing session, and lasts for about five minutes or less. Some of the signals that usher in this phase include: the interviewer glancing at the wall clock, handing back to you your original documents, closing the file, or when he asks his colleagues for their final remarks.

At this point, it's okay to inquire how long you should wait for their response and whether there are more rounds of interviews expected. As you close, stand up relaxed and composed, give the interviewers a firm handshake, and once again thank them for spending their time with you. Smile and create the best final impression of yourself as you leave the interview room.

10

Conducting Follow up

"One's destination is never a place, but rather a new way of looking at things." – Henry Miller

"It's never crowded along the extra mile."
– Wayne Dyer

After attending an interview, it is important that you follow up on the progress and remain in touch with the organization as a way of showing interest in the position. A simple delay in following up can result in missing out on a wonderful job.

The most common way of conducting follow up is sending a thank you letter or an e-mail to each of the interviewers. Alternatively, you can call each one of them to express your gratitude over the phone.

One of the drawbacks associated with calling is that compared to sending mail, a phone call doesn't leave tangible records that can be included in your company file.

Nonetheless, a major advantage of a phone call is that you can get instant updates on the progress being made in the hiring process.

Whichever method you choose, the most effective timing for follow up is immediately after the interview - before final hiring decisions have been made. The importance of conducting follow up at this time is that:

- It places your name once again at the fore of interviewers' minds as they make their decisions on whom to hire.

- It brings you out as a person who has genuinely interest in the job and the company, and thus as a desirable candidate.

- Effective follow up sets you apart as courteous and as a person of exceptional qualities.

A typical thank you letter should bear your address and date, as well as the name, position and address of the recipient. It should also comprise three paragraphs or thereabout.

In the first photograph, thank the interviewer for the interview, and then follow your opening statement with a comment of admiration. This act of attention grabbing will encourage the interviewer to read on.

In the second paragraph, give a summary of something good you learnt from the interview. You can also mention briefly something impressive you learnt about the company, such as the level of professionalism demonstrated by its workers, some of the company's unique business strategies, or any other commendable developments you might have noticed during the visit. This will demonstrate to the interviewers that you have keen interest in the company.

In the third or closing paragraph, do the following two things: express optimism that the company will consider you for the job, and second, volunteer to give any further information that the human resource manager may require concerning your background.

Below is a sample thank you letter illustrating how the above considerations can be incorporated.

Andrew Kemunto

P.o Box 23749 – 123

Kehancha.

12th February, 20__

To

The Human Resource Manager

Kehancha Tea Company

P.o Box 645232 – 123

Kehancha.

Dear Mrs. Agnes Kegoro,

RE: THANK YOU FOR THE INTERVIEW

Kindly accept my thanks for having interviewed me for the Personal Assistant's post last week. You were very ingenious.

As you described to me the opportunities and challenges that come with the position, I appreciated that it calls for very high levels of professionalism. Your brief description of the company's plan to venture into production of green tea for the expansive Chinese and Japanese markets was also very inspiring.

I am optimistic that you will give me a chance to work for your company. I hope to hear from you soon on this. Should you require more information concerning my back ground, kindly let me know.

Yours Sincerely,

Andrew Kemunto.

Rejecting a Job Offer

There may be good times when you will receive multiple positive responses from two or more employers, and courtesy dictates that you explain to either of them why you might not be in a position to take up their offers.

When writing this kind of letter, begin by thanking the manager for extending to you the opportunity, but don't mention anything that could mean his organisation wasn't good enough for you. Instead, give a precise explanation for not taking up the job and end it all on a positive note.

Example of a letter rejecting an offer.

Cecil Dena

P.o Box 32453 – 9089

Nairobi.

17th – Sept – 20__

To:

The Principal

Machweo High School

P.o Box 45324 – 798

Kinago.

Dear Mrs. Obwogi,

RE: REASON FOR NOT TAKING THE JOB OFFER

Thank you for offering me a job as a driver in your school. In July, I had sent my CV and letters of application to a number of reputable companies and institutions for consideration. In addition to your offer, I have received another from a flower firm in my area. Although I had the desire to work for you, I figure out that the latter opportunity will allow me to work from home, which is good for my family.

I appreciate the time that your school's Board of Governors took to interview me and consider my qualifications. You treated me in a courteous and professional way, and I have high regards for your school. I am sorry for any inconvenience I might have caused you and I hope you will get a suitable person soon.

Yours Sincerely,

Cecil Dena.

11

Now that You have a New Job

"When he reached the New World, Cortez burnt his ships. As a result his crew was well motivated."

- The Hunt For Red October

A new work environment can offer you a great opportunity to expand your social and professional networks. It can present to you the opportunity to meet, interact, and form new bonds with people with whom you can exchange ideas and solve problems. A good job can also enable you to pursue other worthwhile goals in your personal and career life.

On the other extreme, a new job can result in anxiety for a number of reasons. For instance, there can never be peace and hope should you realize that the job offers few if any opportunities for growth. Other reasons that could affect your enthusiasm include being required to work for long hours that take away your time for social interactions, or should the organisation turn out exploitative and frustrating in the long run.

Another surprise often awaiting new employees is job insecurity. In some unscrupulous organisations, new employees are laid off after completing the mandatory three months of probation, and if they are lucky, they are asked to re-apply for their positions. This ensures that the employees remain as casual labourers, hence the need to clarify your terms of engagement with an employer right from the beginning.

When confronted with job uncertainties, some people choose to hold on in the hope that the employer will one day be impressed by their dedication and reward them with promotions, pay increments, or improve their working conditions. Others hold on out of the feeling that a job, no matter how exploitative, is better than nothing at all, while the more daring ones seek greener pastures elsewhere.

The number of work-related issues that can crop up in a new environment is beyond the scope of this book, and some of them can only be resolved by enacting laws that offer workers adequate protection from exploitative employers. Nonetheless, a number of important disputes have also been settled amicably by the management through discussions with workers' trade unions.

A Trade Union

This is an organization of workers formed with a view to improve the terms and employment conditions of its members. Compared to individual representation, unions offer better channels through which concerns raised by workers can be presented to employers.

Since the union sends competent negotiators to dialogue with the management, there is often a fair degree of representation and no fear of victimization.

Trade unions are usually financed through members' monthly contributions. Examples of local trade unions include: Kenya Union of Journalists, Food and Allied Workers Union, Kenya National Union of Teachers (KNUT), and the umbrella body of them all: the Central Organization of Trade Unions (COTU).

Avoiding the Last in First out (LIFO) Scenario

As a job seeker, your greatest incentive is to get a stable environment that allows you to exploit your talents and skills to increase your productivity. On the other hand, the employer wants a person who besides being qualified for the job, can also fit well within the company and work as a team with the rest towards achieving the company's goals.

There are, even so, millions of reasons why new employees can be shown the door soon after being hired. Such reasons range from poor time management to alcoholism, absenteeism, and arrogance. Here, we're going to concern ourselves with the three most common reasons relating to work and attitude.

Poor Attitude

Some new employees harbour a sad notion that they will be working with their current employer for a short period of time, after which they will move on to a better paying job elsewhere. Consequently, they show little commitment in their work, assume an air of indifference, and eventually become difficult to deal with. Should the level of productivity of such people decline, or when they become incompatible with the work environment, they get fired.

Whether you are working for a while or for a lifetime with any given employer, commitment to your work is paramount, and so should it remain up to the moment you leave. This is one of the greatest rewards that you can ever give your employer.

Declining Productivity

At the beginning of employment, a new employee is regarded as still learning the ropes and it might take some time before he has gained sufficient experience to work productively.

This learning curve should go up to the point where one's value of production exceeds the amount of salary that he receives. By contrast, any employee whose productivity falls below the amount of his or her salary is seen as a liability to the company, and is thus showed the door. To avoid falling into this trap, do not prolong your learning period unnecessarily. Rather, work hard and let your productivity speak out for itself.

Incompatibility

It's said the grass is always greener on the other side – until you get there! When most people land their most coveted job, for a variety of reasons, they soon realise that it's after all different from what they initially though.

For fresh graduates, they discover that in the real work environment things are done differently from how they were trained in college. When the system falls short of their expectations, many new employees find whining a new hobby, and they criticize everything whenever the opportunity arises.

When the organisation finds it difficult to accommodate the employee, he or she is requested to resign. As a new employee, take it upon yourself to understand the system, its culture and why things are done as they are. Find out the values that are most cherished and adopt them, and at the same time desist from doing what is detested most in the organisation. Socialize freely with your colleagues and try as much as you can to understand your new employer.

Planning for Career Advancement

Despite our craving for more satisfaction and self actualisation at our work places, the corporate pyramid narrows at the top and career advancement becomes a struggle. Understanding this, some organisations provide some kind of movement for their employees in form of succession, promotion or lateral transfers to other departments.

One of the most successful roads to career satisfaction, however, is acquisition of new skills by enrolling for advanced training. Just like in any other worthy undertaking, this requires good planning and timing:

1. Identify a suitable position that you would wish to attain either up your corporate pyramid or elsewhere.

2. Find out what credentials are required for the position and whether you currently qualify.

3. If you indeed qualify, then seize the opportunity and apply for the job if a vacancy already exists.

4. If you do not qualify, find out how you can acquire the required skills, that is, which extra courses you need to pursue and how to finance this worthy investment.

If you're planning to advance within your current organisation, first of all study the company's policy on promotions. Is career advancement based on academic qualifications, nepotism, on-the-job training, experience, etc? This will enlighten you on your chances of forward movement.

Some employers encourage their staff to enrol for advanced training programmes that have a bearing on the company's current or future requirements. Should this be the case with your employer, discuss your training plans with the human resource manager to learn of any available opportunities or those likely to arise in the near future.

Find out from the manager also, whether the company can offer you study leave, scholarship, or fees reimbursement for the course you intend to undertake.

With this information, you can visit a number of institutions offering the course or check out for available online courses on the internet. Enquire about the duration of training, fees requirements and payment arrangements, and whether the training schedule suits you.

Finally, ascertain whether the institution of your choice has financial assistance programmes, and whether you can be exempted from some course units given your academic background, work experience or both.

12

Overcoming Emotional Turmoil

*"The human heart feels things the eyes cannot see,
and knows what the mind cannot understand."*

- Robert Vallett

*"Blaming has no positive effect at all, nor does trying
to persuade using reason and argument. That is my
experience. No blame, no reasoning, no argument,
just understanding. If you understand, and you show
that you understand, you can love, and the situation
will change." - Thich Nhat Hanh*

For most job seekers, the hardest challenge that they have
to overcome is lack of sufficient finances to meet their basic
expenditures such as researching on the internet, mailing
of application documents, registration with job placement
agencies, making phone calls, and transport when attending
interviews.

While some lucky few can rely on their savings or get
assistance from their parents or guardians, the rest have to
do some odd jobs in order to get cash. Indeed, some of the
temporary occupations are not honourable, but most experts

will tell you that the jobs are harmless so long as one doesn't lose their career vision.

By taking this road, you not only boost your financial base which will enable you to reach out to more employers, but you also avoid idleness and being a burden to the people you depend on.

Nonetheless, inadequate financing is not the only source of emotional turmoil for a job seeker. Worry can also result from career setbacks such as an interview that goes wrong, a demotion, or from loss of a previous job. Such situations can result in inability to make proper judgment, poor concentration and loss of self esteem.

All this can have devastating effects on you; especially should you see them as personal failures rather than temporary career setbacks. In order to overcome this and recharge your psyche to keep going:

Accept that you're going through trying times
Accept that job searching is not an easy task, although it is manageable. Accepting too, that life has its own ups and downs, and that what you are going through is a normal process can help you put your priorities right even through the toughest of job seeking times.

Resist the temptation to take setbacks personally
One of a job seeker's greatest challenges is influencing potential employers to think in his or her favour. This can at times prove a Herculean task, especially when the employer's mind is set on who he wants or when competition from other equally qualified candidates is stiff.

In some cases, one may feel as if he has been discriminated against, which can lead to self hatred. In order to lessen the pain coming from such setbacks, you need to be psychologically prepared that winning and losing are two sides of the same coin.

With such a mindset, you shouldn't carry hard feelings with you out of challenging experiences. At any rate, such a mindset will help you to bear realistic expectations and avoid pessimism, desperation, or over confidence in your job search.

Do not panic, relax

In times of life's greatest tragedies, psychologists give this as rule number one: *"do not panic, relax"*. Panic results in more confusion, which makes it hard to come up with sound decisions, and can make you overlook a wide open door out of the crisis.

If you are already in the midst of a job search crisis, relax and sort it out as you would any other problem. Avoid getting emotionally involved, as emotions and reason hardly ever go together.

Resist too, the temptation to tie your identity, self-esteem or sense of fulfilment in life to a prospective job or employer as they can frustrate you.

Build your self-esteem

It is said that confidence and courage two things you can never lose because they are things you can always choose. Self-esteem is largely determined by how people perceive you.

A person with high self-esteem and self-confidence develops a bold approach to life's challenges. Such is the person that employers look for, someone who won't get intimidated by challenges at the place of work.

Face each circumstance with confidence and be determined not to succumb to the setbacks no matter how great they may seem. Above all, put your faith in God and in His ability to find you the way out to a better job.

Maintain optimism and persistence
A strong belief that things will finally work out well for you can help you lessen the emotional stress that could result from a challenging job search. Keep on marketing yourself to more prospective employers even when you receive regrets. As the saying goes, a feint heart never won a fair lady. In the job search process, nothing can take the place of optimism and persistence.

Reach out to someone and discuss the setback
When grappling with a job search crisis on your own, it is easy to exaggerate its magnitude. Reaching out to trusted friends or relatives and discussing with them what you are going through can ease the burden off your shoulders and give you new hope. This kind of openness can also serve as an invitation to these people to assist you in the process. It could also give you a deeper and wider understanding of the situation and perhaps, point to you a way out of the crisis.

Avoid excessive anger
After an unsuccessful interview or after losing a job for whatever reason, avoid emotions of anger. Avoid too, the temptation to sit back and count your losses. Rather, think of how you can develop resilience – the strength and courage to spring back to life.

After a tree stump has been cut down, the plant demonstrates its will to live again by bringing forth more shoots than were initially severed. And when you destroy an anthill, the insects start rebuilding it right there under your feet while you watch!

A person who still hurts from past disappointments, failures or injustices will find it difficult to try again or adapt to a new job. After learning some expensive lessons from your past mistakes and failures, it's time to equip yourself with new job searching skills, pray and move on.

Guard against self pity and substance abuse

No matter how terrible your job loss or search experience has been, resist the temptation to retreat into self pity or alcohol and substance abuse. Self pity makes one feel powerless in the face of challenges. Worse, it consumes the very time and energy that you need to make constructive decisions and chart the way forward in life.

Alcohol and substance abuse, on the other hand, interfere negatively with the one's level of judgment, rationality, and can give you a negative self and public image. Learn to solve your problems with a sober mind, knowing that a good self image is an important ingredient for optimistic approach to life.

Finally, setbacks should turn you into a good problem solver. It is said that it's pressure that makes diamond harder than stone, and that a fool keeps banging his head against the same wall. There is no harm in falling back to jobs you might have previously despised, if only to earn the cash you need to start building your life in the mean time.

When all is said and done, learn to see your circumstances in a positive light. Failure in getting employment could be God's own way of urging you to try your hands at something better, perhaps a business or a talent. True, life is full of opportunities for those who seek them with open minds.

Appendix A

Reasons often given by employers for rejecting interviewees

By reading and understanding the reasons given below why employers turn down some interviewees, you will know what to avoid and what to emphasize on in an interview:

• Poor dressing and appearance.

• Unwarranted show of aggressiveness, superiority complex and know-it-all attitude.

• Poor self-expression due to poor choice of words, poor grammar, or speaking in an inaudible voice.

• Lack of clear career goals and objectives, that is, poor response to the question: "where would you like to be in the next five or ten years in your career?"

• Lack of interest in employment, lack of optimism with the employer, or a show of indifference – a don't care attitude.

• Failure to participate in extra-curricular activities at school or college, which can be viewed as an anti-social trait, lack of self drive, or evidence of being a poor team player.

• Over emphasis on money and other benefits at the expense of work.

• Expecting too much too soon as portrayed in reluctance to start at the bottom of the corporate ladder.

• Lack of courtesy.

• Poor academic records or qualifications.

• Being late for the interview - this shows poor time management.

• Presenting forged or poorly prepared application documents.

• Poor eye contact with panelists during the interview, as it shows insincerity or dishonesty.

• Extreme nervousness, which shows lack of self-confidence and poor preparation for the interview.

• Failure to respond appropriately to the questions asked, giving single word answers, or talking too much.

• Talking ill of your previous employers or teachers. This brings you out as someone still hurting from past injustices. A bitter person often finds it difficult to adapt to new work environments.

• Clear lack of leadership qualities, especially if you are seeking a managerial or administrative position.

• Inability to make important decisions fast enough.

• Unwillingness to relocate closer to the new place of work.

• Questionable listening skills or inability to follow instructions as given.

Appendix B

Some of the most frequently asked interview questions.
The basic reason why interviewers ask questions is to establish how your academic background and previous work experience have prepared you to contribute to what the organisation does. To prove your readiness, formulate short and natural answers to these and more questions when preparing for the interview:

- What are your long and short term career goals and objectives, and how are you preparing to achieve them?

- What do you consider your greatest strengths and weaknesses?

- In what ways do you think you can contribute towards achievement of our company's goals?

- Describe your most rewarding college experience.

- If you were hiring a person for this position, what qualities would you look for?

- What college subjects did you like least and why?

- What college subjects did you like most and why?

- What led you to choose your field of specialization?

- How do you work under pressure?

- What is the greatest mistake that you have ever made?

- What did you learn from the above mistake?

- What major problems have you encountered in school or in your career life and how have you dealt with them?

- Are you willing to spend at least six months as a trainee?

- Are you willing to travel?

- Are you willing to relocate?

- What two things are most important to you on the job?

- How would you describe the ideal job for you?

- What part time or attachment jobs have you been most interested in and why?

- What qualities should a successful manager have?

- Describe the relationship that should exist between a supervisor and those reporting to him or her.

- What two or three accomplishments have given you most satisfaction? Why?

- What do you think it takes to be successful in a company like ours?

- What do you expect to be earning in five years?

- How would you describe yourself?

- What motivates you to put forth your greatest effort?

- Who are you?

- What are you?

- Tell me about yourself.

• In what school activities have you participated? Why?

• What do you think determines an individual's success in a work situation?

• Do you consider yourself a leader or a follower? Why?

• Define cooperation.

• What will be the most difficult aspect of making a transition from college or your last job to our organization and Why?

• What kind of work environment do you prefer?

• Why should we hire you?

Recommended Websites

"Opportunities to find deeper powers within ourselves come when life seems most challenging." - Joseph Campbell

Though it would not be practical to list all the good sites on the internet in this space, we have nonetheless endeavoured to bring you some of the most recommended sites, especially those with contents relevant to local situations.

Feel free to send us suggestions of other useful sites so we can include them in our future editions of this book. Our contact email address is: *excellencemedia@live.com*. We hope your will find these links useful.

www.vts.intute.ac.uk/acl/tutorial/jobsearch
If you are new to online job searching, I would recommend that you start here. This site is a basic tutorial on how to make your first online job search systematic and productive.

www.ke.tiptopjob.com
An online recruitment resource for both jobseekers and advertisers. You can search both local and international jobs by category depending on your line of profession. Registration is free, after which you can upload your CV for local and international employers to head hunt you.

www.learn4good.com/jobs/language/english/search_
resumes/country/kenya
This is by far, one of the most current and comprehensive sites to conduct your job search.

Jobs are listed by profession, eligibility criteria, as well as the specific local town where the job is located, e.g. Nairobi, Naivasha, Kisumu, Eldoret, etc.

www.kazipoint.com
A career site featuring jobs of companies who use Kazipoint Recruitment Management System. Registration required for new users, though the service is free of charge.

www.linktoalljobs.com
A premium employment search engine that puts jobseekers in control in finding the right job on the internet.

www.linktoalljobs.com
A professional Human Resources, recruitment, selection, outsourcing and manpower sourcing company.

A great resource for Kenyans seeking jobs both locally and internationally.

The website's career toolkit section is a great place to learn more about the job search process free of charge.

www.casualjobskenya.com
An effective resource for candidates and recruitment agencies searching for job placements or seeking temporary, causal as well as permanent vacancies. The site lists opportunities arising countrywide.

www.brightermonday.com
A new and free service for East Africa. The site's resume database saves you from having to upload your CV every

time you make a job application. This is a great way of taking advantage of modern technology in your job search.

www.nationmedia.com/careers
Nation Media's official website's careers page. Here you will find job postings from reputable organisations in Kenya.

www.monster.com
One of the world's leading resume databases and job search sites. This is good for those seeking international jobs.

www.hotjobs.yahoo.com
This is Yahoo's job search service. Loads of important information on the job search process as well as a good site to hunt for jobs outside the country.

References

Andersen R.E., *Essentials of Personal Selling: Then you professionalism*, 1995, (ties – hall, New Jersey

Andrew J. W., *Bouncing Back: How to stay in the game when your career is on the line*, 1992, McGraw-Hill, New York

Borjas. G. J., *Labour Economics*, 1996, McGraw-Hill, New York.

Burchill. F., *Labour Relations*, 1992, Macmillan, London.

Carmicheal K., 'Saints and Sinners' *New Society*, 75 (7 February): 1986.

DesmondW. Evans, *People, Communoication and Organisations*, 1986, Pitman, London.

Ellen Cassey and Caren Nussbaum, *9 To 5: The Working Woman's Guide to Office Survival*, 1983, Penguin Books.

Stanford F. & Dauwarlder P.D., *Communicating in Business: An Action-Oriented Approach*, 1994, Austen Press & Irwin.

Hayatt and Linda Gotlieb, *When Smart People Fail: Rebuilding Yourself for Success*, 1988, Penguin Books, New York.

Patricia A. & Yeandale S., *Youth Unemployment and the Family: Voices of disordered times*, 1992, Routledge, London.

Richard H.B., *The Resume Kit*, 1984, John Willey & Sons, New York.

Shuller H. R., *Life's not fair but God is good: How to turn life's challenges into personal triumphs*, 1993, Bantam Books, New York.

The Adam's Resume Almanac, 1994, Adam's Publishing, Holbrook Massachusetts.

www.ingramcontent.com/pod-product-compliance
Lightning Source LLC
Chambersburg PA
CBHW070523030426
42337CB00016B/2085